Thanks, Dad

from _____

_____

Thanks, Dad

ST. MARTIN'S PRESS

NEW YORK

ALSO BY ALLEN APPEL

Thanks, Mom
From Father to Son

Editor: Jared Kieling
Production Editor: David Stanford Burr
Design: Henry Sene Yee

ISBN 0-312-15221-3

10 9 8 7 6

Thanks, Dad

THANKS DAD,

for . . .

_____

Getting up
in the night to walk the floor when
I was a baby.

Feeling guilty when
Mom got up to walk the floor when
I was a baby.

THANKS DAD, *for...*

Staying in bed and
getting your sleep so you could put in a
full workday and bring home the paycheck
that kept the wolf from the door and the
landlord at bay. And maybe feeling
a little guilty that Mom had to get up
and walk the floor when
I was a baby.

THANKS DAD, *for...*

────────────

Getting burped on and not
really minding.

Admiring me.

Changing the occasional diaper.
When you couldn't get
out of it.

THANKS DAD, *for...*

_____

Teaching me to
walk, talk, eat solid food,
drink from a cup, and other
basic life skills.

Carrying me when I was tired.

Holding me when I was afraid.

THANKS DAD, *for...*

_____

Rocking me to sleep.

THANKS DAD, *for...*

_____

Checking for monsters under the bed.

Reading to me
at night,
until
you
fell
asleep.

THANKS DAD, *for...*

———————————

Telling me you loved me.

Showing me you loved me even when
you didn't say it.

THANKS DAD, *for...*

———————————

Sitting up with me when I was sick.

Ripping off my Band-Aids real fast

so it wouldn't hurt.

It hurt anyway.

_____

Teaching me to:

Ride a bike

Roller-skate

Throw a ball

Catch a ball

Keep my eye on the ball

Kick a ball

Hit a ball

Teaching me to
construct and eat:

Radish and butter sandwiches
Mustard on pretzels
Sugar on lettuce leaves
Peanut butter on celery
Peanut butter on bananas
Peanut butter and mustard sandwiches
Peanut butter and sweet pickle sandwiches

THANKS DAD, *for...*

Working all day and still taking time to
play with me at night.

THANKS DAD, *for...*

———————

Letting me cry when I was hurt.

Showing me how to get hold of myself when
I was too big to cry.

And not making fun of me while
you were doing it.

THANKS DAD, *for...*

_____

Taking me:

For drives in the country

On picnics

On hikes

For ice cream

To the movies

Letting me sit on your lap and
steer the car.

THANKS DAD, *for...*

_____

Teaching me how to:

Whistle

Cross my eyes

(They never got stuck, Mom.)

Wriggle my ears

Wink

Impressing on me the dangers of
putting my tongue on metal pipes when
the weather was below freezing, hanging my
head out the window of a rapidly
moving car, playing with matches,
broken glass, wild animals that act weird,
and strange adults offering
candy and car rides.

Thanks Dad, *for . . .*

_____

———————————

Taking out
a hundred splinters.

Applying
a thousand bandages.

Driving me to
the emergency room.

Holding my hand.

THANKS DAD, *for...*

Attending:

Soccer games
Band concerts
School plays

And suffering in silence at
all of the above.

THANKS DAD, *for . . .*

M aking me
take
piano lessons.

Letting me
quit
piano lessons.

_____

Playing games with me.

Never
letting me cheat.

Not
letting me win on purpose.

Teaching me:

Not to be afraid of a little blood
To get right back up after falling down
Never to give Mom any back talk

Yelling at me:

When I ran out in the street

When I got bad grades

When I didn't do what Mom said

When I didn't do my homework

When I needed it

Teaching me to:

Tell the truth

Admit it when I was wrong

Be kind to smaller kids

Being fair.

Admitting you didn't know everything.

(Even though I thought you did.)

Thanks Dad, *for...*

Showing me, by example:

How to stand up for myself
To not let anyone push me around
To take care of my sister and my brother
To not let anyone, ever, say anything bad
about my mother

THANKS DAD, *for...*

Allowing me to have:

A dog

A cat

A hamster

Goldfish

THANKS DAD, *for* . . .

Making me learn
to take care of all of my pets.

(But cleaning up after them sometimes
even though it was my job.)

Many costly trips to the vet.

THANKS DAD, *for...*

———————————

Showing me that
I should not to be afraid of:

Strange dogs

Bugs

Snakes

Teaching me how to cook:

Eggs

A steak

Spaghetti

Not much else

_____

Teaching me to:

Try as hard as possible

Never give up

Make do with what I've got

Accept what I cannot change

Improvise, when necessary

Get myself out of trouble

THANKS DAD, *for...*

R escuing me.

On a number of occasions.

Building me a tree house.

Showing me what's poison ivy
and what's not.

(Leaves of three, let it be.)

THANKS DAD, *for...*

———————

Getting up
in the middle of the night
to come to my room and kill the:

Mosquito

Cricket

Monster

THANKS DAD, *for . . .*

———————————

Teaching me not to show off,
grandstand, or play to the crowd.

Explaining and showing that the
best way to act in most situations was to
just be myself.

Saying you were sorry when you
were wrong.

THANKS DAD, *for...*

Letting me help when you were
working around the house.

Asking for my help
when you really didn't need it but you
wanted to teach me
something.

Making me help.
Sometimes you really needed me,
sometimes you didn't,
but I almost always learned something.

Letting me get dirty.

Cleaning me up when I got dirty.

THANKS DAD, *for...*

Teaching me
to earn my own money.

Making me save my money.

Letting me spend my money when it
was important to me.

Teaching me to pay my own way,
to pay what I owe, and that money was
important
but that it didn't necessarily bring
happiness.

Teaching by word and example that
all people are equal.

Climbing up onto roofs and into trees
to retrieve various balls, Frisbees, and sundry
other flying objects.

Trusting me.

Enduring, without complaint:

Homegrown plays

Talent shows

Questions without end

Long,

involved funerals for small animals,

both wild and domestic

Making me:

Pull weeds
Paint the porch
Shovel snow
Clean my room

Clean up after dinner
(sometimes)
Wash the dishes
(every once in a great while)

THANKS DAD, *for...*

_____

Letting me dream.

Laughing.

Not laughing.

Shelling out money for
all sorts of lessons.

Loaning me money when I needed it.

Not loaning me money when I thought
I needed it,
but really didn't.

THANKS DAD, *for...*

Helping me build interesting
science projects.

THANKS DAD, *for...*

Teaching me how to:

Pound a nail

Sand a piece of wood

Paint, without getting it all over myself

Clean up

Telling me stories about when you
were a boy.

Letting me swim in the river
even though
Mom was sure I'd get bit by a snake
or catch polio.

Teaching me to be
curious, confident, capable, and
calm.

THANKS DAD, *for* . . .

─────────────

Making me visit
all those boring
aunts and uncles and relatives
so I would know
my family.

Being interested
in my family's past, and
passing that interest
along to me.

Dragging me to:

Museums

Caves

Battlefields

State Parks

Family reunions

_____

Making me take good care of my teeth
and go to the dentist
every six months.

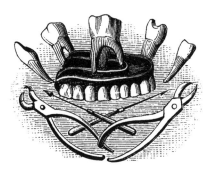

Teaching me how to study.

THANKS DAD, *for...*

Teaching me a couple of nifty tricks.

Making me many things—
bookshelves, beds, toys, and tables,—and
showing me that the best things in life
are homemade.

Your patience.

Rescuing the hamster from
the heating duct.

Helping me with my homework.

————————————

Always remembering my birthday.

Teaching me good manners.

Being funny.

THANKS DAD, *for...*

———————————

Thanks Dad, *for...*

_____

Helping me carry heavy loads.

Knowing when I wanted to be
left alone.

Knowing when I needed a
helping hand.

THANKS DAD, *for...*

Fixing all the broken toys.

Bringing back presents when you
went on trips.

THANKS DAD, *for...*

———

All the barbecued steaks, burgers, hot dogs, chickens, and flaming marshmallows.

Listening carefully.

Taking time.

Being calm.

Setting limits.

Convincing me in a nice way that
getting a weird haircut wouldn't really be a
good idea.

THANKS DAD, *for* . . .

———————————————

Having faith in me.

Being there,
night and day, year after year.
Always.

THANKS DAD, *for...*

_____

Teaching me the names of:

Birds

Bugs

Trees

Flowers

Putting together,
(some assembly required)

all those:

Christmas presents

Birthday presents

Bicycles

Tents

Swing sets

Electric trains

P utting up the Christmas lights

on the house.

THANKS DAD, *for...*

_____

Putting up and remembering

to water

the Christmas tree.

Encouraging me to use my
imagination.

Taking me trick or treating.

THANKS DAD, *for . . .*

———————————

Teaching me to be good.

(most of the time)

THANKS DAD, *for...*

_____

Letting me be bad.

(some of the time)

THANKS DAD, *for* . . .

Letting me read comic books
and watch a reasonable amount of TV.
See,
it didn't rot my brain after all.

THANKS DAD, *for...*

———————————

Teaching me:

To do my best, win or lose
To give people a second chance,
and realize that everyone makes mistakes

(Even you!)

To do what I say I'm going to do.

THANKS DAD, *for*. . .

_____

Teaching me to drive a car.

Not yelling at me

(too much)

while you were teaching me
to drive a car.

THANKS DAD, *for...*

Showing me how to take care of a car.
And for those driving tips.
(You can always take a curve
ten miles an hour faster
than the sign
says.)

Letting me use the family car.

Not yelling at me when
I wrecked the car.

(twice)

(not my fault, either time)

(honest)

Letting me have a beer at home when
I was old enough.

THANKS DAD, *for . . .*

_____

Not criticizing
my dates.

Not embarrassing me
in front
of my friends.

_____

Explaining, *(badly)* the facts of life.

THANKS DAD, *for...*

Making me
take a job every summer and
all through college.

THANKS DAD, *for...*

———————

Taking me to work with you.

Letting me make my
own mistakes.

Not making fun of me
or making me feel bad after I made
the mistakes.

THANKS DAD, *for...*

———————

Showing me how
to finish
what I start.

Showing me how
to start over
when necessary,
without regrets or
recriminations.

THANKS DAD, *for...*

Standing:

In front of me
       when there was danger
Up for me
       when I was right
Beside me
       when I was married
Behind me
       when I made up my mind

THANKS DAD, *for...*

Helping me see
and appreciate nature:

The transcendent beauty
of fall
The soft green hope
of spring
The warm joy
of summer
The cold clarity
of winter

THANKS DAD, *for . . .*

———————————

Thank you for making me

WHAT I AM.

THANKS DAD, *for*...

_____

_____

_____

_____

_____

_____

Thanks Dad, *for...*

_____

_____

_____

_____

_____

_____

_____